The Birth of Israel Exhibit

The Birth of Israel Exhibit

Rabbi Joshua Stampfer,
Institute for Judaic Studies and
Israel Jubilee Committee Member

Standing at the Western Wall, Jerusalem, 1947

During the summer of 1947 we knew that momentous changes were just beyond the horizon. The United Nations had dispatched a Special Commission on Palestine to determine the feasibility of a solution to the Jewish - Arab conflict by partitioning the land into two entities. That same summer my wife, Goldie, and I set sail on the Marine Carp for a year of study in Jerusalem at the Hebrew University. I was a student at the Jewish Theological Seminary and this was to be a year of immersion into Judaic Studies.

It turned out to be the most significant year of our lives. On November 29, 1947 the United Nations General Assembly, meeting at Lake Success, New York, voted to partition Palestine and to create a Jewish and Arab state. In Jerusalem, we shared in the incredible joy that swept through the city at the announcement that after two thousand years of exile and persecution, a Jewish state had come into being.

The joy was short lived as seven Arab nations attacked Israel intent on destroying this state at its very birth. I joined the Haganah and participated in the defence of a besieged Jerusalem and the eventual victory that assured the survival of the State of Israel. These photographs recall the hardships and the wonders of those days. They serve to remind us of the sacrifices that had to be made before Israel could he secure. They convey to us in eloquent colors the hopes and dreams of a people who longed to become the masters of their own destiny in their ancient but ever new homeland.

For my generation this exhibit evokes a heroic past. For younger generations it conveys a deep appreciation for all who made Israel possible. For all of us, it is a prayer of Thanksgiving in living color, that we were privileged to share in this miracle.

2900 SW Peaceful Lane, Portland OR USA 97201 • (503) 246-8831

Historic photos © Marlin Levin, Jerusalem - all rights reserved
Contemporary photos © Chanan Getraide, Kvutzat Schiller - all rights reserved
Catalogue design © Israel Jubilee - all rights reserved
Production: Gefen Publishing House Ltd., Jerusalem
This catalogue or any portion thereof, may not be reproduced in any form or by any means, electronic, mechanical, photocopying, recording, or stored in any retrieval system of any nature without written permission from the publisher, Israel Jubilee.

The Color of Time

The Photography of Marlin Levin

One of photography's inherent characteristics is its ability to capture and record moments in time and preserve them for posterity. Historic photographs are always moving and fascinating, as they bring back to life past events witnessed by a third party, but also enable the viewer to have a first-hand experience of the happening at the instant it occurred.

The photographs of Marlin Levin possess the qualities both of historic documents as well as of a moving testimony to the years around the proclamation of the State of Israel. Many a picture was taken during these years, however, Levin's photographs are unique in more than one dimension, as they have also captured the "color of time," in the only known color transparencies made at the time, which were miraculously preserved in excellent condition to this day.

Born in Harrisburg, Pennsylvania, Marlin Levin decided to follow a career in journalism. His studies at Temple University were interrupted by World War II, during which he served in Europe and Japan, and graduated with honors after his return. He immigrated to Israel in August 1947 and was immediately hired as an editor for the *Palestine Post* (now the *Jerusalem Post*) where he survived the bombing of the building in February 1948. As a working journalist, over the years he has reported on most of the major events that took place in Israel as correspondent for *United Press*, *ABC* and *London "Daily Mail."* In 1958 he founded the *Time-Life* bureau and currently is correspondence for *LIFE* in Jerusalem.

Marlin Levin's color photographs are an instantaneous record of events, gestures and expressions, a chronicle of the incidents and happenings of the period. Although he was trained as a journalist, his images taken from the very moment he set foot in Palestine in 1947, are mostly devoid of pathos and sensationalism, and are imbued with kindness. They are endowed with sensitivity; with an eye for the human factor, and filled with emotion: the emotion of the eye behind the camera discovering a new country, often full of pride and enthusiasm; at times naive and childlike, looking in wonder at the people, the views and scenes of the state yet to come.

Levin's visual records of the historic moments of the pre-state period and the years following the proclamation of Israel, are invaluable documents and preserve for posterity yet another chapter of our national history.

Nissan N. Perez,
Horace and Grace Goldsmith,
Curator of Photography
The Israel Museum, Jerusalem

The Birth of Israel Exhibit

"Idiot, Idiot!"

Those were the first words spoken to me when I arrived with Betty, my bride of six weeks, in Jerusalem in September, 1947. The epithets came from the mouth of a boy standing outside the bus that had brought us from Haifa Port. How could he have known that I had just arrived from the U.S.? The parting words of our friends and family in New York were not dissimilar — "Are you crazy! Going to Palestine at a time like this? You must be mad. Wait until the situation settles down."

Well, it never did settle down and had we listened we never would have gone to Israel where we have spent most of our lives without so much as a boring day.

But back to the boy outside the bus. It was only later that I realized he was not really screaming "Idiot!", but waving a paper in my face yelling, "Yediot", the name of a newspaper he was trying to sell me.

Few Americans went to Palestine in those days. We were idealists, not lunatics. We had come to help create a Jewish state. On arrival, we found a nasty, three-way conflict in progress. Arab was fighting Jew, Jew was fighting Arab, and both were fighting the British. The British were following a policy of divide and rule, but by mid-1947, were losing the battle and soon would retreat.

Extremists on all sides seemed to dictate our lives. Arabs would shoot up Israeli buses and bomb Jewish centers, strew nails on roads over which British diplomats traveled. Israelis would throw grenades into cafes frequented by British soldiers, spray Arab villages with gunfire, and blow up bridges used by the British military. There were British who collaborated with the Arabs in killing Jews and there were British who would supply Jews with weapons. A crazy-quilt life of gunfire, arson, assassinations that went on 24 hours a day.

In preparation for our trip, we thought we had prepared for every eventuality: mosquito netting, a two-way radio, books, kitchen ware, and a good supply of Kodachrome film, relatively new on the market, for my 35mm camera.

I took my first pictures with a box camera at the age of eight and became serious about photography while serving with the U.S. forces in Europe during World War II. As a professional journalist, I never went anywhere after that without my portable typewriter and my camera.

What attracted my camera lens in those chaotic days in Palestine was not so much the blood and thunder of the tri-partite war, but the ordinary people who suffered through it without a whimper. I never quite understood how they, or rather we, could live the lives we did. Constant curfews, searches, zoned-off areas, outbursts of terrorism — approaching all

Photo by Betty Levin, 1997

with such aplomb, even nonchalance. Nothing seemed to faze us. We would walk smilingly through the streets of Jerusalem, accepting the situation as it was, going about our daily affairs with a supreme air of confidence (even when hand-to-hand fighting was only blocks away) and greeting each other with one standard phrase: "Yehe'ye tov"! In effect we were saying, "Don't worry, good days are ahead."

Shortly after arriving in Palestine, Betty and I went on a tour of the country, traveling by rickety bus, donkey cart, trekking always over bad roads, and sleeping in tents in the kibbutzim. Everywhere we lugged our knapsacks, typewriter and camera.

Back In Jerusalem, I went to work for *The Palestine Post* and *United Press*. I shall never forget my indefatigable editor, Gershon Agron, with whom I daily walked to work during the siege. One day, as we neared Zion Square, not far from our editorial offices, shells began to explode around us. I shouted to him to get to the nearest shelter. He refused and instead went to have his shoes polished by an elderly shoe shine man sitting exposed under a cinema marquee. Later, I asked Agron why he did such a foolish thing. He replied, "If that old man was brave enough to sit out there while shells fell, then I could do nothing less but
to oblige him."

One day at the end of November, while Betty and I were visiting a children's village up north, we heard that the U.N. had decided to partition Palestine. That meant the creation of a Jewish state! In one stroke the international community had reversed nearly 2,000 years of history.

We returned to Jerusalem to see the entire city in a glorious mood. Spontaneous processions filled the downtown streets. It was almost dark, but I lifted my camera and through the viewer saw a truck filled with jubilant youth, one of them waving a blue & white flag. It was a scene out of *Les Miserables*. I clicked away.

Even during the height of the Arab siege of our city when we were without water, electricity, fuel and food, the average Jerusalemite, weary and hungry, displayed good humor — even when they went for their meager rations or traded a bit of bread for an extra pail of water.

In the editorial room of *The Post*, we would spend nights producing a paper under difficult conditions. When the British shelled our building with 25-pounders, we would take our typewriters and crawl under tables to edit copy. We went to work each day famished. To ease the pangs of hunger, we ripped pages from American magazines advertising delicious foods. One night we saw on the bulletin board a photograph of a huge ham. "Hey," yelled one of our sub-editors, "take that down! That's not kosher!"

Then the day in 1949 arrived when the fighting stopped, although in Jerusalem it continued even after the armistice agreements were signed. For years, Jordanians guarding the wall of the Old City would periodically subject us to sniper fire, and because of that, Jerusalemites walked down main streets behind hastily constructed fire walls.

In May, 1949, the entire city turned out to see for the first time its military forces on parade. These were the men, women, and even animals, who won the war against unbelievable odds — a citizens' army in the truest sense. No one stayed home. Proud people filled every available spot in the streets and on buildings.

I aimed my camera at the crowd, at the faces of the men and women marching, at the idealistic boys and girls on a truck waving a Zionist banner. It was a day that made Israelis feel they were invulnerable, for if they could conquer the armies of six nations, they could do anything! And, historically speaking, they did.

Viewers of this exhibition will note that I have not chosen to show pictures of fighting. I rather chose to do what few others have done: to portray a people in the act of creating a state, and in the process, going about their daily business. Simple, ordinary people, many of them newly-arrived, all of them caught up in the maelstrom of history, carrying out superhuman tasks, suffering deep privations, and laughing it off with a "Yehe'ye tov!"

To me, they were the heroes whom I hoped to capture for posterity on color film — they and the lives they led. May their spirit never die...

Marlin Levin,
Jerusalem

The Birth of Israel Exhibit

The Birth
of Israel
Exhibit

A State is Conceived

The Birth
   of Israel
Exhibit

In a scene reminiscent of revolutionaries of the French Revolution, these ecstatic flag-waving Zionist youth acclaim the U.N. decision to partition Palestine into a Jewish and an Arab state. The night before, November 29, 1947, the Special General Assembly meeting at Lake Success had made reality of Theodor Herzl's prediction in Basel, in 1897, that a state would be established in 50 years. Here as dusk settled on King George Street in a spontaneous outburst of joy, cheers mixed with tears. On the morrow, as David Ben-Gurion had expected, war would begin. But this day was given to euphoria.

Today, King George Street is heavy with traffic but little has changed.

All Contemporary Photos by Chanan Getraide

The Birth
of Israel
Exhibit

Ecstatic people choke the streets of Jerusalem in the late afternoon of November 30, 1947, to herald their independence after nearly 2,000 years of subservience to foreign rule. Not knowing how to react, some stood silent, bewildered, incredulous, and watched history take shape.

The Birth
   of Israel
Exhibit

Here, a British supernumerary policeman joins Scouts on Jerusalem's Jaffa Road in a parade that formed spontaneously to celebrate statehood.

The Birth
of Israel
Exhibit

British
Surrender
Mandate

The Birth
   of Israel
Exhibit

In the wake of a number of Arab attacks on Jewish settlements, a British policeman warns an Israeli to leave his home in the Talbieh Quarter of Jerusalem. "When we pull out," said the constable, "you will be massacred by the Arabs." The Jerusalemite remained and later became a diplomat in the Israeli Foreign Service. In the background, barbed wire marks off the peaceful Jewish-Arab neighborhood as a protected zone, and to the extreme left, stands the wall of Old Jerusalem. The British were out of the country by May, 1948.

The same scene nearly 50 years later on what is now Jabotinsky Street. Barbed wire dividing the street was removed when the British departed in May, 1948. Apartment buildings and trees today obscure the view of the Old City of a geographically united Jerusalem.

The Birth of Israel Exhibit

Zionism's Triumph

The Birth
of Israel
Exhibit

"We Were Born to be Free -- For a Life of Creativity and Labor" reads a sign on a truck bearing idealistic Zionist youth in Jerusalem celebrating Israel's founding.

The Birth of Israel Exhibit

In 1947, a Jewish farmer in Yavne rehabilitates a devastated land in the fulfillment of the Zionist ideal.

The Birth
of Israel
Exhibit

Who We Were

War Correspondent Julian Meltzer, later a Vice President of the Weizmann Institute of Science, drives one of the few cars available in Jerusalem in 1948.

The Birth
of Israel
Exhibit

The Birth of Israel Exhibit

Nazareth in September, 1947, seemed as if it had not changed since biblical times.

The Birth of Israel Exhibit

A common form of transportation in Palestine in 1947 was on bicycle or on foot. Here a Jew travels to Jerusalem's Mahane Yehuda market on his horse.

The Birth
of Israel
Exhibit

This Arab in Tiberias travels his route on a donkey while others must walk. Only the well-to-do could afford cars in 1947.

In the mystical town of Safad in 1947, this pious Jew heads for morning services at one of the many centuries-old synagogues.

The Birth of Israel Exhibit

The Birth of Israel Exhibit

No longer a popular street to stroll, King George Street is one of Jerusalem's main thoroughfares, home for the Great Synagogue, hotels, supermarkets, a department store, fast food eateries and high-rise apartment buildings.

Unconcerned by the trouble brewing between Jews and Arabs, these nuns from a nearby convent, enjoy a stroll on a hot autumn afternoon in 1947 on Jerusalem's King George Avenue.

The Birth
of Israel
Exhibit

Siege of Jerusalem

The Birth of Israel Exhibit

In the center of Jewish Jerusalem where Ben-Yehuda Street meets King George Avenue, the Haganah set up a roadblock manned by a guard who immigrated from the U.S. in 1948.

This busy corner in downtown Jerusalem controls traffic on an east-west, north-south axis. The roadblock of 50 years ago has long since given way to gridlock during peak traffic hours. The guard later returned to Philadelphia.

All walls are down. Where once Jerusalem residents rushed by, fearing snipers' bullets from the Old City, now beautifully landscaped Independence Park in center city has replaced the barricades. The walls were removed when the city was geographically unified by the Six-Day War in June, 1967.

The Birth of Israel Exhibit

Shooting from the Old City of Jerusalem, only a few hundred yards from the downtown area, forced quick construction of this wooden wall in 1948. When the war was over, the sniping continued and it was replaced by a concrete wall.

The Birth of Israel Exhibit

Jaffa Road looks much the same after 50 years except for the crowds and, of course, the heavy bus traffic.

During the siege of Jerusalem, the city's main streets were devoid of traffic and people. Jaffa Road, seen here, normally would be bustling with shoppers and vehicles, but during the siege, there was no merchandise, gasoline or food. These pedestrians defied intermittent shelling to reach their destinations.

The Birth of Israel Exhibit

During the siege, Ben-Yehuda Street in Jerusalem was nearly empty except for a boy selling magazines and a few brave shoppers. On February 22, 1948, the entire street was demolished by three trucks loaded with TNT. It was the worst terrorist incident in Israel's history with nearly 200 dead or wounded.

Probably no single street in Jerusalem has changed so much as has Ben Yehuda, now a bustling pedestrian mall with smart shops and outdoor cafes.

The Birth
of Israel
Exhibit

Arab Siege of Jerusalem

Hunger

The Birth of Israel Exhibit

The siege stopped nearly all but essential work in Jerusalem. With no electricity, no fuel, little food or water, Jewish population dropped to below 70,000 in 1948.

The Birth
of Israel
Exhibit

Hunger stalked the city and some were close to starvation, forcing men and cats to hunt for scraps in nearly empty garbage cans. A popular staple was a weed growing in the fields similar to dandelion.

The Birth
of Israel
Exhibit

In 1948, during the siege, rations in Jerusalem sometimes consisted of only a few noodles each day. This housewife poses demurely before putting them into a new American pressure cooker. Without fuel, she cooked atop a wood fire in her garden. On the way to get her skimpy rations, a shell fired by the Arab Legion from the Old City nearly killed her.

50 years later, still living in Jerusalem, she is planting instead of cooking.

The Birth
of Israel
Exhibit

Normally bursting with produce, Mahaneh Yehuda (Camp of Judah) market in Jewish Jerusalem was empty of both food and shoppers during the siege in 1948.

Tourists now find Mahaneh Yehuda market one of the most colorful, frenzied sites in the city. Local shoppers buy there because of the high quality, abundance and relatively inexpensive prices. The best felafel in town is available here from kiosks.

The Birth of Israel Exhibit

Arab Siege of Jerusalem

Thirst

The Birth of Israel Exhibit

With their men away, these Jewish housewives from the upscale Jerusalem neighborhood of Rehavia cheerily carry their family's daily ration of water into the house. With the pipeline to Jerusalem cut, the city had to depend on wells for its supply. Water was distributed from tank-laden trucks.

For some, a pail of water per person per day was not enough. In 1948, this woman barters a rare piece of bread for water from a monk sitting by the tap of his monastery's private well.

The Birth
of Israel
Exhibit

The Birth
of Israel
Exhibit

The New State

The Birth of Israel Exhibit

A United Nations negotiated truce lifted the siege of Jerusalem on June 11, 1948. It was then that the underground Haganah could show its colors as the newly formed Israel Defense Forces. At a ceremony on a school playground in war-ravaged Jerusalem, the Chief Rabbi of Israel, Isaac Halevy Herzog, in top hat, presented the colors to Jerusalem Army Commander, David Shaltiel. General Shaltiel trained in the French Foreign Legion. When the war was resumed one month later, Israeli forces took the initiative, and in bitter fighting defeated the Arabs.

Jerusalem, a city of flags, began to repair the 1948 war damage even before the war ended. Here the construction is being done outside the Consulate of Iran on Balfour Street, which was home to many foreign diplomatic missions. The flag of Iran is no longer seen in Jerusalem.

Some Jerusalemites spent the June, 1948 cease-fire to move to safer quarters. Porters used any vehicles they could find. Here, one crate carrying household goods once held shells and fuses.

The Birth of Israel Exhibit

The Birth
of Israel
Exhibit

The policeman is long gone and the empty lot next to the house with the red roof is one of hundreds of gardens that have been planted in the past 50 years.

One of Israel's first policemen to be seen after the State was founded in May, 1948. Seen here directing "traffic" on Jerusalem's Ussishkin Street.

The Birth
of Israel
Exhibit

Protest

The Birth of Israel Exhibit

In the summer of 1948, U.N. Mediator, Count Folke Bernadotte of Sweden, tried to make peace by offering large parts of Israel to Arabs. Extremist members of the small LEHI underground demonstrated outside the Belgian Consulate-General where Bernadotte held talks with Israelis.

Balfour Street, in the swank Talbieh neighborhood, was once known as the Street of the Consulates, the most imposing of which was the Belgian. It is still there, but most of the others have left, including the Swiss, the Turkish and the Iranian. Today, Balfour Street houses the official residence of Israel's Prime Minister.

Arriving for a meeting with Israelis, Bernadotte (front left in white cap) peers at protestors. Days after this picture was taken, in September, 1948, LEHI members assassinated him and his French aide (behind right) a few blocks from this site.

The Birth of Israel Exhibit

The Birth
 of Israel
Exhibit

Relief

In Safad, an elderly woman carries home a package sent by her relatives abroad.

The Birth of Israel Exhibit

The Birth of Israel Exhibit

Food is no longer collected in packages sent from abroad on Lunz Lane; it is now served at outdoor cafes. In the background the bank building is fully restored on Ben-Yehuda Street.

In Jerusalem of 1949, food parcels from the U.S. relieve the torment of hunger, while in the background, bombed-out Ben-Yehuda Street is being rebuilt.

The Birth
of Israel
Exhibit

As war passes, the first water arrives in Jerusalem, filling rooftop tanks.

The Birth
of Israel
Exhibit

A Nation
Unified

The Birth of Israel Exhibit

Off Tel Aviv's shore in mid-1948, the Irgun Zevai Leumi ship *Altelena*, carrying arms for IZL forces, was fired upon and sunk by Haganah forces on orders of David Ben-Gurion. By his action, Ben-Gurion unified the armed forces and prevented civil strife. The Irgun under Menachem Begin turned the military organization into a political party called Herut.

The Birth
of Israel
Exhibit

First Independence Day Parade

One year of statehood had passed. It was now May 4, 1949. Israel was not at peace but it had signed armistice agreements with three of its principal foes: Egypt, Lebanon, and Jordan. Syria was still two months off. But the first Arab war against the Jewish State had ended. Masses of immigrants inundated the State. Elections had been held. Income tax had been initiated. El Al was flying. Food was severely rationed. The national Treasury was empty. "Yihye Tov" (It will yet be good) was the popular salutation.

Despite all, there was reason enough to celebrate Israel's first Independence Day. None of Jerusalem's swelling population stayed home that day. They overflowed the streets; climbed lamp posts, stood on every balcony.

A half century of wear and pollution from vehicular traffic have taken their tolls on this once striking structure in downtown Jerusalem.

The Birth of Israel Exhibit

A mid-century cross section of Jerusalem's population line the streets to watch their men and women parade on Israel's first Independence Day. Virtually everyone had a relative or a close friend in the lineup.

Here they come, led by massed Israeli flags.

The Birth
  of Israel
Exhibit

These are the foot soldiers who broke through the Arab siege and kept most of Jerusalem safe for Israel during the State's War of Independence. Once a ragtag army, here they show off their new helmets and uniforms.

The Birth of Israel Exhibit

Women soldiers fought along side the men during most of the war. Here, on Israel's first Independence Day, the women of the army march proudly as the crowds cheer.

The Birth
of Israel
Exhibit

The army that won independence for Israel in 1948 was now showing itself for the first time. What Jerusalemites saw that day in early May were proud men and women soldiers marching albeit out of step, World War II armored cars, the Fire Brigade, nurses in white, Kibbutz pioneers and the transportation corps' mules lugging artillery. A bizarre scene from a bygone day at a time when war had already entered a nuclear and jet era. But the mules went where vehicles could not and in the end, that is what helped to win the war.

World War-vintage armored cars were few, but they made a strong impression on the enemy.

The Birth
 of Israel
Exhibit

Assemble, Israel!

The Bible (Deuteronomy 31: 10-13) enjoins Jews to assemble every seven years... "men, women, children and the stranger..." to hear the reading of the Law of Moses. Soon after the establishment of Israel, the Jews of Jerusalem gathered in a sports field to observe their first "Hakhel" and to hear readings from the Torah.

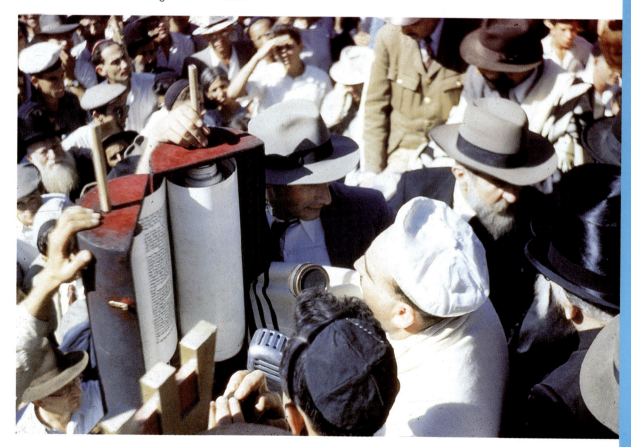

The Birth of Israel Exhibit

The Birth
of Israel
Exhibit

A New Era

In 1952, in the temporary Knesset building in downtown Jerusalem, Yitzhak Ben-Zvi takes the oath of office as President, following the death of Chaim Weizmann. A photo of Theodore Herzl, founder of modern political Zionism, dominates in the background.

Jerusalem, 1952. An extraordinary gathering of Israel's political elite outside the temporary Knesset building. To the right of Prime Minister David Ben-Gurion (center) is Premier-to-be Golda Meir. Among the others are Knesset Speaker, Joseph Sprinzak (front), Cabinet Ministers, Haim Moshe Shapiro (right of guard), Dov Joseph (right of Golda), Joseph Burg, white-haired Pinchas Lavon, and Deputy Speaker, Binyamin Mintz (far right). They wait to greet Israel's newly-elected President, Yitzhak Ben-Zvi.

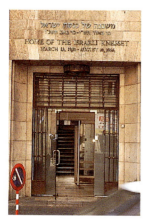

The Frumin Building was originally built to house a bank. It never did. The Knesset, after holding its first meeting in the Jewish Agency hall in Jerusalem on February 14, 1949, moved to a converted cinema in Tel Aviv. In December, 1949, the Knesset returned to Jerusalem and the Frumin building where it remained until 1966.
Today, it is the home of the Ministry of Tourism.

The Birth of Israel Exhibit

The Birth
of Israel
Exhibit

Immigration

The Birth
of Israel
Exhibit

At the Port of Brooklyn, New York, anxious families bid farewell to the few American men and women who emigrated to the new State by ship... a 14-day journey. In the 1940's, planes were not a common form of transport overseas.

The Birth of Israel Exhibit